After Dinner JOKES

After Dinner JOKES

MICHAEL O'MARA
BOOKS LIMITED

First published in Great Britain in 1995 by
Michael O'Mara Books Limited
9 Lion Yard
Tremadoc Road
London SW4 7NQ

A CIP catalogue record for this book is available from the British Library

ISBN 1-85479-704-2

1 3 5 7 9 10 8 6 4 2

Designed by Robert Updegraff

Printed and bound in Singapore

THE DIRECTOR, Peter Hall, asked each member of the cast of the National Theatre's production of *Oedipus* to say what frightened them most. Sir John Gielgud strolled to the front of the stage and said: 'We open in two weeks.'

THE LADY in the hospital bed was feeling better and had enjoyed her dinner - until two nurses rushed in and looked at her in alarm. 'For goodness sake,' said one to the other: 'It's too late to tell her now - she's eaten it!'

POPE BENEDICT XIV was dying. His eyes opened for the last time and he saw two cardinals peering at him and said: 'Thank you Lord for allowing me to die like you between two thieves.'

JUDGE to old lag: 'Smith! You here again!'

Old lag: 'What's good enough for you, M'Lud is good enough for me!'

* * *

TOMMY COOPER said to the waiter: 'Have you got frog's legs?' 'Yes,' the waiter replied. 'Well then,' said Cooper, 'hop over the counter and get me a cheese sandwich.'

* * *

'MY UNCLE Joe's dead.'
'No he isn't - it's just a story he puts around to gain sympathy.'

* * *

IMMIGRATION OFFICIAL Sydney, Australia: 'Have you any criminal convictions?'

Hopeful immigrant: 'I didn't know you still needed them.'

* * *

DO YOU KNOW THE STORY of the caterpillar who, seeing a butterfly fly by remarked: 'You'll never get me up in one of those.'

* * *

A FRENCHMAN and an Irishman were to be guillotined. The Frenchman went first but was reprieved when the blade stuck just six inches above his neck. Before the Irishman lay his head on the block he said: 'Hold on a moment. I think I can fix it.'

* * *

MOSES SAID, as he came down from Sinai: 'The good news is I've got it down to ten. The bad news is Adultery is in.'

* * *

'THE OTHER NIGHT I looked at a lady's hand and knew immediately she was going to be lucky.'

'How could you tell?'

'She had four aces.'

* * *

'I ASKED my doctor to tell me the bad news but he said he would prefer to send the bill by post.'

* * *

'CAN WE TRUST the city any more when the future of invest seems to be investigation?'

* * *

BEHIND every successful man there stands an amazed woman.

* * *

MY WIFE said to me in bed last night: 'Do you believe in free love?'
I said: 'Certainly not!'
She said: 'Then, that'll be ten pounds.'

* * *

A MAN walks into the bank to cash a cheque and the cashier says: 'You will have to identify yourself.'
The man looks in the mirror and says: 'Yes, that's me all right.'

* * *

KING GEORGE V gave the following advice on carrying out official duties: 'Never miss a chance to relieve yourself; never miss a chance to sit down.'

* * *

SIR JOHN GIELGUD'S many gaffes include: On meeting Herbert Marshall, the one-legged British actor in California - 'Ah, Herbert, foot-loose in Hollywood, I see.'

* * *

AND: To a TV interviewer in St Louis, Missouri - 'Claude Rains. I don't know what happened to him. I think he failed and went to America.'

* * *

AND: On on being told by an actor that a fellow actor had a chip on his shoulder because he was a failure responded: 'Well, you're a failure but you haven't got a chip on your shoulder.'

* * *

MICKEY ROONEY, the diminutive actor, was said to have approached a chorus girl with the words: 'Let's make love.'

To which she responded: 'All right but if I ever come to hear of it I will be very cross.'

* * *

EVELYN WAUGH was asked by a fan at a public dinner for his autograph. He obliged. The excited fan went back to his table and read what Waugh had written: 'Go away.'

* * *

GRAHAM GREENE received a cable from his American publisher who had just received the manuscript of his new novel: 'Loved the story; hated the title.'
Greene cabled back: 'Easier to change publisher than title.'

* * *

US NEWSPAPER PUBLISHER to his Washington correspondent: 'Send all the details. Nevermind the facts.'

* * *

CHICAGO'S MAYOR DALEY was never good with the press and his aide said on one occasion: 'Print what he means, not what he says!'

* * *

NEW YORK CITY'S Mayor, Jimmy Walker: 'We are launching this innovation for the first time.'

* * *

GETTING THINGS WRONG: George Raft on being offered the part of Rick in *Casablanca* - 'Who's ever heard of Casablanca . . . I don't want to star opposite an unknown Swedish broad.'

* * *

'IF WE MAINTAIN our faith in God, our love of freedom and superior global air power, I think we can look forward to the future with confidence.

General Curtis LeMay, February 1956

* * *

I BELIEVE we are on an irreversible trend towards more freedom and democracy. But that could change.

Vice-President
Dan Quayle

* * *

MY IDEA of a good dinner is first to have good food, then discuss good food, and after this good food has been elaborately discussed, to discuss a good topic - with myself as the chief conversationalist.

Winston Churchill

* * *

EATING MY WORDS has never given me indigestion.

Winston Churchill

NOTHING is so exhilarating as to be shot at without result.

Winston Churchill

* * *

TOBACCO is bad for love; but old age is worse.

Winston Churchill

WHEN I WAS YOUNGER I made it a rule never to take a strong drink before lunch. It is now my rule never to do so before breakfast.

Winston Churchill

A MAN gets drunk at a party and his friends call a cab to take him home. Once in the cab the man starts to tell the cabby about his life: how lonely he has been since his wife left him, how hard his job is, how no one appreciates him.

'You seem like a nice guy,' the drunk says.

'Yeah,' says the cabby indifferently.

'What do you say? Do you think there's room in the front seat for a pizza and a couple of six-packs?'

The driver thinks about it for a minute and says, 'Sure, why not?'

'Gee, thanks,' says the drunk, leans over the partition and throws up.

* * *

A NEW TEACHER asks his class: 'Who knocked down the walls of Jericho?'
Jones responds: 'It wasn't me, sir.'
Appalled at the level of ignorance, the teacher goes to see the headmaster: 'I asked "Who knocked down the walls of Jericho?" and Jones says he didn't do it.'
'Well,' said the headmaster if he says he didn't do it then I believe him!'

A CAR knocks over a hare. The driver and passenger get out and see that the hare is in a bad way - covered in blood and hardly breathing. 'Wait a minute,' says the driver, 'I've got something in the car which might do the trick.'

He gets a spraycan from the car and begins to spray the hare. To the passenger's amazement the hare gets up, runs a few steps and appears to wave at the driver. Then it runs a few more steps before stopping to wave again.

'Good heavens!' exclaimed the passenger. 'What did you spray the hare with?'

'Hair restorer with permanent wave,' came the reply.

* * *

SIR STANLEY UNWIN was dining with a foreign publisher who offered him a cigarette. Sir Stanley rejected the offer saying: 'I tried it once but didn't like it.' At the end of the meal the foreign publisher suggested a brandy. Sir Stanley refused: I tried it once but didn't like it'. Next day, Sir Stanley introduced the foreign publisher to his son. Quick as a flash the foreign publisher quipped: 'Your only son, I take it?'

ON BEING TOLD that they couldn't film Lillian Hellman's play *The Children's Hour* because it concerned lesbians, Goldwyn said: 'O.K. We make it with Albanians, then.'

* * *

THE FAMOUS CONDUCTOR Sir Thomas Beecham used in his early days to go round conducting regional orchestras taking with him only the leader of his orchestra and first violin. Some of the orchestras they visited were not very good and on one occasion Sir Thomas leant forward as he was conducting and quipped to his friend: 'Don't look now, but I think we're being followed.'

WHEN the Spanish dictator General Franco was on his death bed he asked in a feeble voice who were the men weeping in the corner of the room. 'They are your Generals, sir, come to say farewell.' 'Where are they going?' Franco asked.

* * *

NOEL COWARD was asked why he drank champagne for breakfast. 'Doesn't everyone?' he replied.

OPENING a Red Cross bazaar in Oxford Noel Coward began, 'Desperately accustomed as I am to public speaking.'

* * *

A MAN was a speechwriter for a famous politician whom he hated. One day he had his revenge for years of writing platitudes. Half-way through a long speech, which the politician had no time to read before he delivered it, the speechwriter printed in big letters, 'You pompous idiot. Now make up the rest yourself!' There followed only several sheets of blank paper.

TWO IRISHMEN were out shooting ducks. One took aim and shot one which fell to the ground. The other Irishman said: 'Why did you waste a shot? The fall would have killed it?

* * *

TWO IRISHMEN are sitting in front of the TV watching a cowboy film. Towards the end of the film the bad guy is riding furiously toward the edge of a cliff pursued by the sheriff.

One of the Irishmen says: 'I'll bet you fifty pounds he rides over the cliff and kills himself.'

'You're on,' says the other Irishman.

The bad guy rides over the cliff and is killed. The second Irishman hands over fifty pounds.

'I feel a bit guilty,' says the first 'because I've seen the film before.'

'So have I,' said the other Irishman. 'I just didn't think he would be stupid enough to do it again.'

ON A ONE NIGHT STAND the woman praised her lover for being so active. 'Well,' smirked the man, 'that's because I've been in the VD clinic for the last six weeks.'

'Oh yes?' she replied. 'What's the food like? I'm going in tomorrow.'

* * *

SAM GOLDWYN'S SECRETARY asked him if she could destroy files over ten years' old. 'Sure,' he said. 'But keep copies.'

* * *

EPITAPH: Here lies Captain Ernest Bloomfield accidentally shot by his orderly, 2 March 1879. Well done good and faithful servant.

* * *

MAKING HIS WAY along a crowded railroad platform in Rome, Goering happened to collide with an Italian aristocrat. The nobleman demanded an apology. 'I am Hermann Goering,' snapped the marshal.

'As an excuse that's not enough,' replied the Italian coldly, ' but as an explanation it is ample.'

IN THE FOYER of a big hotel Beecham saw a distinguished-looking woman whom he thought he knew. He paused to talk to her and vaguely remembering she had a brother asked her whether he was still working at the same job. 'Oh, he's very well,' she said. 'And still king.'

* * *

WHEN AN AMERICAN humourist visited Venice for the first time, he cabled his editor: 'Streets full of water, please advise.'

* * *

GROUCHO MARX sent a telegram to the exclusive Friar's Club in Hollywood to which he belonged: 'Please accept my resignation. I don't want to belong to any club that will accept me as a member.'

* * *

A TIPSY MAN lumbered up to Groucho, slapped him on the back and said, 'You don't remember me, do you?' Marx glared back at him and replied: 'I never forget a face but in your case I'm glad to make an exception.'

* * *

Returning to the text

C *(Summarising)* Ask the children to retell the story in one or two sentences.

C *(Clarifying)* Ask: *What is a 'funny bone'?* Explain if necessary.

W Look at pages 2–3. Find 'tree' on page 2. Ask: *What letter has been added to 'tree' on page 3? Why?*

W On the same pages, ask the children to tell you the words with 'ee' in them. ('tree', 'week' and 'keeper')

C *(Clarifying)* Ask the children to list the tools and equipment the characters used to plant the trees.

Group and independent reading activities

Objective Extend their vocabulary, exploring the meanings and sounds of new words (7.2).

C Write the following words on pieces of card: 'shed', 'stream', 'pond', 'bridge', 'swing', 'hole'.

- Ask each child, in turn, to pick a card, read the word by sounding out the phonemes and then find it in the story. They then read the sentence with the word.
- Ask the children to tell you what the word means.

Assessment *(R, AF1)* Are the children able to read the words outside the context of the book?

Objective Know that print carries meaning and, in English, is read from left to right (7.1).

- Prepare photocopies of the following unfinished sentences for each child:

  The children _______ to the park.
  Everyone wanted _______ give trees.
  Dad put _______ by the shed.

She put it by_______ pond.
Floppy gave _______ bone.

- Ask the children to read the sentences and guess what word would make sense in the gaps (they are all high frequency words).
- Ask the children to fill in the missing words and then check their sentences with those in the book.

Assessment *(R, AF3)* Can the children guess the words easily without looking at the book? Do the children reread the sentences after writing in the missing word?

Objective Explore and experiment with sounds, words and texts (5.1).

W With the children look at the labels on the trees. Help the children to work out what the tree names are, writing them down letter by letter and attempting to work them out using their phonic knowledge.

- Do any of the children recognise some of the tree names?
- Provide books on trees for the children to check what they look like or bring in leaves of the various trees for the children to draw around.
- Draw a table on the board with two columns headed 'character' and 'tree'. With the children's help fill in the columns, e.g.

Character	Tree
Dad	oak

- Ask the children to write sentences saying who planted what, e.g. 'Dad planted an oak tree'.

Assessment *(R, AF1)* Are children confident in attempting to work out new words?

Speaking, listening and drama activities

Objective Speak clearly and audibly with confidence and control and show awareness of the listener (1.4).